ECO-
ARTS & CRAFTS

Written
by
Stuart A. Kallen

Published by Abdo & Daughters, 6535 Cecilia Circle, Edina, Minnesota 55439.

Library bound edition distributed by Rockbottom Books, Pentagon Tower, P.O. Box 36036, Minneapolis, Minnesota 55435.

Edited by Julie Berg
Cover Photograph, Vic Orenstein
Interior Photographs, Vic Orenstein

Special thanks to the **Target Earth™ Kids,** Jennie, Libby, Joe, Ted, Kenny & Grace.
Artistic Consultant, Patti Marlene Boekhoff

Library of Congress Cataloging-in-Publication Data
Kallen, Stuart, 1955–
    Eco-Arts & Crafts / written by Stuart A. Kallen.
        p.   cm – (Target Earth)
    Includes bibliography, glossary and index.
    Summary: A collection of craft projects which use art supplies made from recycled materials and things found around the house.
    ISBN 1-56239-208-5
    1. Handicraft–Juvenile literature.   2. Nature Craft–Juvenile literature.   3. Recycling (waste)–Juvenile literature. [1. Handicraft   2. Recycling (waste).   3. Nature craft.]
I. Title.   II. Title Eco-Arts & Crafts.   III. Series.
TT160.K25   1993
745.5–dc20   93-19059
                                                                              CIP
                                                                              AC

DISCLAIMER: The activities in this book should be safe when conducted as instructed. The author and publisher accept no responsibility for any damage caused or sustained due to use or misuse of ideas contained herein.

 Thanks to the trees from which this recycled paper was first made.

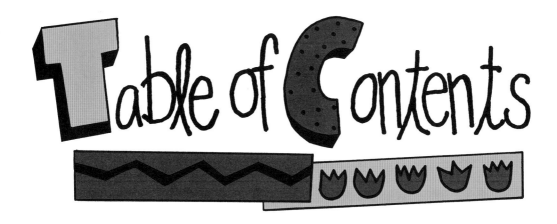

Table of Contents

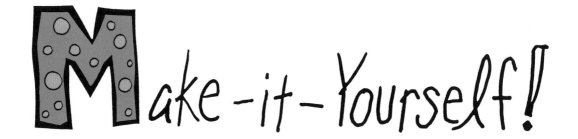

Make-it-Yourself!

Anybody can go to the mall and buy paint, paper, and art supplies. All it takes is money and time. But factories that produce some types of paint also produce toxic waste. And most paper is made from trees that were once growing in a forest. Even worse, almost all of that stuff comes wrapped in plastic—which goes straight to the landfill.

You can buy your art supplies at the store. But you can have a whole lot of fun, save money, and help save the Earth, if you make them yourself. If everyone did it, there would be more forests and less garbage. And most importantly, you would have a better time. Think about it. If you make your own paint, you can mix up special colors that are yours and yours only. You can even name your colors after yourself—Bobby Brown, Ashley Orange, or Sue Blue.

When you use homemade paint on handmade paper, it will be the only picture like it in the world. Using a little science and a lot of creative spirit, you can make some great art.

You can also express yourself with recycled materials. Instead of taking out the trash, transform the trash. You're only limited by your imagination. Some say recycled art is the wave of the future—so get on that wave and ride!

Paint from the Planet Earth

Some of the first artists in the world (that we know about) made paint from minerals, dirt, and water. Using cave walls for canvases, ancient artists drew pictures of jungle cats, reindeer, bison and horses. With iron oxide, a naturally occurring mineral, cave painters mixed up a vibrant red paint. With charcoal, they made a deep, rich black. With brushes made from fine twigs, the artists left their mark with masterpieces that are still beautiful 30,000 years later. You too can mix up some earth colors and leave your mark—just like those ancient cave people. Maybe someone will be marveling over your earth art in the future!

If you want to make great earth paint you have to become a soil explorer. Stop thinking of earth as mud or dirt, but as color base. Look for colored minerals in the dirt out in the woods. Check out cliffs, study stream beds, and research under rocks. Earth isn't all brown, but many colors, from brick red to green to black. Become a doctor of dirt, a master of mud. Some other places to look for colored dirt are construction sights (be careful!) and roadsides that are cut through hills. Try to find many samples of different colors of earth. Scrape them up and collect them in old jars. Avoid sand and look for stuff that makes a nice, pasty mud.

Once you collect your dirt you need some materials to turn it into paint.

- Old pans
- Plates or flat pans
- A cup
- Water
- Dirt
- Paintbrush
- A round rock or rolling pin
- An old screen, sieve
- A spoon, putty knife, or fork
- A bowl or plastic milk container with the top cut off

Step 1 Spread the dirt out on a plate or flat pan and leave in the sun until it is nice and dry.

Step 2 Pick out rocks, gravel, twigs, etc.

Step 3 If you want to be like the cave dwellers, crush the dirt up with a round smooth stone. If that's too hard for you, use a rolling pin.

Step 4 Using a screen, sieve, or flour sifter, sift the dirt into a bowl or cut milk container. This will make the dirt into a fine powder.

Step 5 Pour a few spoonfuls of the powdered earth into a cup. Add enough water to make a thin paste. Mix the paste with a putty knife, spoon, or fork. Add water until the paste is as smooth as paint.

Step 6 Use a paint brush to make your mark on rocks, paper, or sidewalks.

Juicy Spicy Colors

For brighter colors, mix food spices into your earth paint. Chili powder is dark red. Curry powder is gold. Turmeric is yellow-orange. Powdered oregano is green. Powdered drink mixes come in many colors and will add color to your earth paint.

For other colors, use grape juice, tomato juice, or orange juice instead of water. Experiment!

Paint with Eggs

Some of the greatest paintings in the world are painted with egg yolks. It's true! The paint is called egg tempera, and if it's properly made, it can last thousands of years without cracking or fading. Egg tempera paintings from ancient Greece and Rome are still with us today.

The trick to making egg tempera is separating the egg yolk from the white. If you don't know how to do that, ask someone who does to show you how.

- Eggs
- Vinegar and water
- A fork
- Paper towels
- Jars with screw-on tops
- Spices or powdered drink mixes for color
  (see Paint from the Planet Earth page 5 for colors).

To make each color:

Step 1 Separate egg yolk from egg white.

Step 2 Place yolk on a paper towel and roll it around CARE-FULLY until the outside of the yolk is dry and free from any egg white. Yolks break easily, so be careful.

Step 3 Put the egg yolk in one hand and gently pick it up by pinching it between with your thumb and forefinger.

Step 4 Hold the egg yolk over the jar and prick the bottom of it with a fork. Drain the yolk into the jar. Throw away the yolk skin.

Step 5 Using your fork, mix in spices, drink mixes or a few drops of juice until you get the color you want. Mix well.

Step 6 Add a few drops of vinegar and a few drops of water.

Since you need to use one yolk for every color you want, you will probably become an egg-spurt at yolk separation. To save on yolks, plan to paint with a couple of friends. There should be enough paint to do several paintings.

When painting with egg tempera, you need to use a lot of water on your brush. Egg tempera dries quickly, so only make as much as you need for one painting session.

Painting with egg tempera can be fun!

Make Your Own Paper

The people of the United States use 50 million tons of paper every year. That means cutting down 850 million trees—every year! Add the rest of the world's paper use, and billions and billions of trees are cut down every year—just for paper. Those are trees that can no longer produce oxygen and clean the air we breathe. It also makes millions of animals homeless, when their forest home is chopped down, chopped up, and carted away. But we can make our own paper from old newspapers, rags, and lint. It takes a little time and effort, but it's fun, and will make your artwork unique.

Paper is made up of millions of tiny fibers. When paper is made, it starts out as 99 percent water and 1 percent fiber. When it is finished it is about 90 percent fiber and 10 percent water.

When paper is made from wood, trees are chipped up into tiny pieces. The pieces are mixed with water and strong (polluting) chemicals. The mixture is boiled until it becomes a thick goo called slurry. The slurry is poured onto a wire mesh where the water is pressed out by heated rollers. The end result is paper. When you make your own paper, you follow this same process, only on a small scale—and without the chemicals.

Recycled Paper Paper

- Old newspapers
- Two buckets
- Water
- A blender or egg beater
- A rolling pin
- Old, clean plastic bags
- Cornstarch
- Measuring cup and spoons
- A piece of screen or a mesh "spatter shield." Note: A splatter shield is used to cover pans while bacon is frying. It works great for paper-making and can be found at most hardware or housewares stores.

Step 1
Tear newspaper into tiny pieces and place them in a bucket.

Step 2
Add water to cover all the paper and let stand for at least two hours.

Step 3
Using a measuring cup, fill blender with the newspaper mixture and blend until it is a smooth slurry. Add more water if needed. After the mixture is slurry, pour into a fresh bucket. Repeat until all the paper mixture is slurry.

Step 4
Add three tablespoons (45 ml) of cornstarch to the slurry and stir.

Step 5
Dip the screen or splatter shield into the slurry until it is covered evenly.

Step 6 Lay the screen down on spread out newspapers.

Step 7 Cover the screen with an old plastic bag and roll hard with a rolling pin.

Step 8 Hang up the screen where it can dry.

Step 9 When dry, carefully peel the paper off the screen.

Making recycled paper.

Candle Wax Finger Crayons

Lots of people love to burn candles. But sometimes they don't use the whole candle and they end up with a half-burned stub. That stub usually gets thrown in a drawer somewhere and is forgotten. You can turn old candle stubs into crayons, making your own personal colors.

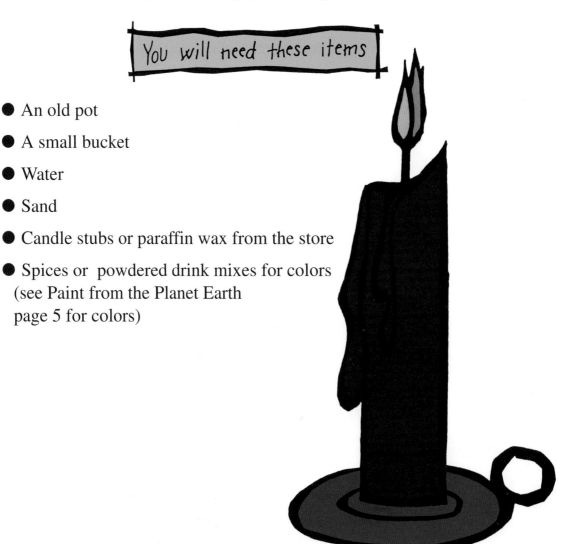

You will need these items

- An old pot

- A small bucket

- Water

- Sand

- Candle stubs or paraffin wax from the store

- Spices or powdered drink mixes for colors
  (see Paint from the Planet Earth
  page 5 for colors)

To make crayons:

NOTE: Get permission to use the stove or work with someone who does.

Step 1 Moisten sand with water until it is thick enough to make sand castles.

Step 2 Pour sand into a small bucket and pack tightly.

Step 3 Stick your finger into the sand and pull it out, making sure no sand fills in the hole. Do this with several fingers. This will be the mold for your crayons.

Step 4 On the stove, over a very low heat, melt old candle stubs or paraffin in an old pot.

Step 5 To color your crayons, add colored spices or powdered drink mix to the paraffin.

Step 6 Slowly pour the liquid wax into the finger holes in the sand.

Step 7 Let dry for several hours.

Step 8 Remove crayons from the sand and color away.

 Glue It Yourself

Glue is so easy to make that you'll never get stuck without it. You won't be in a bind, and you can be secure that if you cement these ingredients together you're in for a fasten-ating experience.

- Flour
- Sugar
- Water
- A wooden spoon
- A small saucepan
- A wide-mouth jar with a tight lid

NOTE: If you are not allowed to use a stove, ask someone to help you.

Step 1 In the saucepan, mix one tablespoon (15 ml) of flour with four tablespoons (60 ml) of water.

Step 2 Add one teaspoon (5 ml) of sugar.

Step 3 Place the saucepan on the stove and turn on a very low flame.

Step 4 Stir mixture constantly until it is thick. Remove from heat.

Step 5 Spoon paste into jar and cover tightly until needed.

Homemade paste only lasts a few days. Soon mold will start to grow in your jar. For fun, you can look at the mold close-up with a magnifying glass or under a microscope.

Mobile-ize

A mobile is a hanging sculpture whose pieces gently turn with the movement of the air. You can make mobiles out of things you find in forests or meadows, or you can make them out of stuff in the recycling bin. The trick is getting everything to hang right and balanced.

You will need these items

- Tree branches that are 12 to 36 inches (30 to 90 cm) OR

  An old broom OR mop handle

  an old yard stick OR even long coat hangers.

- Yarn, twine, ribbon, and/or string

- Pine cones, seashells, small rocks, wildflowers, fruits, nuts, feathers, or any other interesting things you want to hang from your mobile.

~NEXT~

Step 1 Tie about 12 inches (30.4 centimeters) of string, ribbon, yarn or twine to each end of the tree branch, broom handle, or yard stick.

Step 2 From the end of each string, tie shorter sticks.

Step 3 Tie more ribbon, string, etc., to the ends of those sticks.

Step 4
Hang pine cones, interesting rocks, fruit, or nuts from the ends of those strings.

Step 5
For a trash mobile, hang jar lids, cardboard tubes, styrofoam trays cut in interesting shapes, and magazine pictures glued on cardboard from the crossbars. Use wire hangers instead of wood for crossbars.

A mobile is a hanging sculpture.

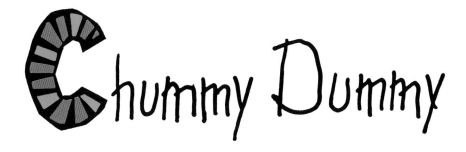

Chummy Dummy

You can make a life-size buddy out of used clothes and old newspapers. This is fun for Halloween or any time of year.

You will need these items

- Newspapers
- String or twine
- Safety pins
- Old shirts, pants, gloves, socks, and shoes
- Balloons or a watermelon or pumpkin

~NEXT~

Step 1 Stuff the pants and shirt full of crumpled up newspaper.

Step 2 Tie the leg and arm holes shut with string so the paper doesn't fall out.

Step 3 Pin the bottom of the shirt to the waistband of the pants with safety pins.

Step 4 Stuff gloves with shredded paper and then pin to the arm-holes of the shirt.

Step 5 Stuff socks with shredded paper and pin them to the leg-holes of the pants.

Step 6 Put shoes on the socks.

Step 7
Use a balloon, watermelon or pumpkin for a head. Draw a face on the balloon. If you're using a watermelon or pumpkin, use a carrot for a nose, and pepper slices for ears.

Step 8
To make a lightweight, realistic head, see the next project.

Chummy-dummy and friends.

Mask About It

Life-size masks that fit over your head? Sure thing! With paper-maché (ma-SHAY) anything is possible. Now aren't you glad you masked?

You will need these items

- Large balloons
- Clay
- Tape
- Newspapers
- A bucket or large bowl

- Flour
- Water
- A spoon
- Scissors
- Paint

NOTE: This is a messy project. Wear old clothes and find a place where no one will mind the mess (outdoors, the basement, the garage, etc.).

Step 1 Find a balloon that, when blown up, is larger than your head. Blow it up.

Step 2 Think of the balloon as a head. Make lips, a nose, eyebrows, and ears out of clay and stick them onto the balloon. You can even make hair out of clay. If the clay won't stick, use tape to hold it onto the balloon.

Step 3 Mix even amounts of flour and water together in a bucket or large bowl. Stir with a spoon until mixture is smooth.

Step 4 Dip shreds of newspaper in the flour mixture until they are soaked.

Step 5 Apply the soaked newspaper strips to the balloon.

Step 6 Layer the newspaper onto the balloon until it is covered. Leave a space at the stem of the balloon. The more newspaper layers, the stronger the mask will be.

Step 7 Let the paper-maché dry for at least one day.

Step 8 Paint the mask.

Step 9 Pop the balloon.

Step 10 Cut a hole in the bottom of the mask so that it fits over your head.

Step 11 Cut out eyeholes so that you can see while wearing the mask.

Step 12 Cut out small holes for your nose and mouth.

Step 13 Wear the mask or use it as a head for the chummy dummy in the last project.

Paper-maché can also be used for puppets and sculptures.

Trash City

You can build your own city in which you can play with your trains, dolls, or cars. And since it's made out of trash, you can make it as big as you want. What are you going to name it? Jason-apolis? Chris-burg? Sue City?

You will need these items

- Clean used cans
- Plastic bottles
- Paper
- Used paper bags
- Old magazines
- Fabric scraps

- Scissors
- Tape and glue
- Sheets of cardboard or plywood
- Rocks, small pine branches
- Paints, magic markers, colors
- Used boxes from cereal, soap
- Tubes from paper towels, bath tissue

Step 1 Construct houses and high-rise buildings out of the used cans, plastic bottles, used boxes, and cardboard tubes.

Step 2 Glue paper, old bags, or magazine pictures around the cans, boxes, and jars.

Step 3 Use the fabric scraps, paint, and magic markers to decorate the buildings with windows, doors, etc.

Step 4 Glue the buildings onto a large sheet of cardboard or plywood.

Step 5 Use small branches for trees and glued gravel for roads.

You can fill your city with toy cars, trucks, dolls, or trains.

Totem Poles

You can make totem poles to tell a story or as decoration.

You will need these items

- An old log, dry and clean
- Paint
- Glue

~NEXT~

Step 1 Paint designs and faces around the log.

Step 2 Glue on pebbles, moss, and leaves to decorate the designs and faces.

Step 3 With permission from an adult, carve designs into the wood.

NOTE: You could also use an old cardboard tube instead of a log for a totem pole.

Totem poles tell stories and make fun decorations.

Picture This

A bunch of pictures glued into one picture is called a collage (ko-LAHJ). When you coat them with a glossy finish, it's called découpage (DAY-koo-pahj). If you do this project you can become the Wizard of Ahj!

You will need these items

- White glue

- A paint brush

- A large sheet of heavy cardboard

- Old magazines, newspapers, photographs, tin foil, and old wrapping paper

OR

For a nature collage, use leaves, ferns, dried flowers, and other things from the outdoors.

~NEXT~

Step 1 Think of a theme such as animals, rock bands, or whatever you like. Cut out many pictures from magazines, newspapers, and photographs that fit with the theme.

Step 2 Use a paint brush to coat a sheet of cardboard with white glue.

Step 3 Paste down all the pictures you have cut out. Arrange them in interesting shapes. Fill in spaces with old wrapping paper and tin foil.

Step 4 Use a paint brush to coat the entire collage with a layer of white glue. Let dry.

Step 5 Coat the collage again. The glue should dry hard and shiny.

Use pictures from magazines and newspapers to make a collage.

Stamp It Out!

Vegetables make interesting designs when used as stamps. Use them as they are, or carve something into them.

You will need these items

- Paper
- Paint and a paint brush
- A knife
- And any or all of
  - Corn on the cob
  - Broccoli
  - Apple
  - Potato
  - Cauliflower

Step 1

Make designs by putting paint on corn and pressing it onto paper. Do the same with broccoli, cauliflower, cabbage, or whatever plant or vegetable you like.

Step 2

Cut apple or potato in half and carve your name or a design into it. (Children should get parental help with using a knife)

Step 3

Apply paint to the design on the potato or apple and stamp it onto paper.

Stamp your own design using potatoes or apples.

 o Dye For

Tie-dyed shirts never go out of style. In fact, tie-dying is a very old art that dates back many centuries. Ancient examples of tie-dyed cloth have been found in South America, India, Japan, and China. Many countries in West Africa have a tradition of making beautiful tie-dyes including Sierra Leone, Ivory Coast, Ghana, Togo, Senegal, and Nigeria.

For a natural look, you can make your own dyes from plants and berries. In this project, you will learn to make dyes for tie-dying clothes.

 o make your own dye:

You will need these items

- A cooking pot
- A large bowl
- A measuring cup
- A stove
- Jars with lids
- A strainer
- A spoon
- Water

Tie-dye is always in fashion and a lot of fun to make.

For coloring your dye use plants and berries

Plant	Parts to Use	Color
Beets	leaves and roots	red
Blackberries	berries	purple
Blueberries	berries	bluish-purple
Cranberries	berries	red
Dandelion	flowers	greenish-yellow
Elderberry	berries	lavender
Grapes	fruit	purple
Lily of the Valley	leaves	light green
Onion (yellow)	skins	light brown
Onion (red)	skins	rust
Oranges	fruit and skins	orange
Raspberries	berries	pink
Spinach	leaves	green

 NOTE: Get permission to use the stove or work with an adult.

Step 1 Gather together plants that you need.

Step 2 Chop plants or squish them in a bowl.

Step 3 Use at least one pint (.5 liters) vegetable matter for each quart (1 liter) of dye you are making. Use even more for richer color dyes.

Step 4 Put at least one part vegetable matter to two parts water into a cooking pot. Cover.

Step 5 Bring the mixture to a boil on the stove.

Step 6 After the mixture comes to a boil, lower heat and simmer for one hour, stirring occasionally.

Step 7 Remove from heat and cool.

Step 8 Strain out vegetable matter.

Step 9 Pour dye into jars.

Magic Wand

- A stick or dowel rod about 12 inches (30 centimeters) long
- Colored paper or cloth scraps
- Scissors
- Ribbon
- Glue

To make a magic wand:

Step 1 Cut two layers of cloth or paper about 5 inches (15 centimeters) square.

Step 2 Put the two pieces of cloth or paper together and cut them into a five-pointed star.

Step 3 Glue the edges of the stars together. Leave one end open.

Step 4 Let dry overnight.

Step 5 Stuff a small amount of paper or cloth into the open end of the star. This will give it a puffy appearance.

Step 6 Put the end of the stick into the open end of the star.

Step 7 Glue the star shut around the stick. Let dry.

Step 8 Tie ribbons around the stick.

Step 9 Add glitter or bows to your magic wand.

Magic wands are always fun to make!

Rub-a-Dub-Dub

Plants, leaves, and flowers come in all shapes and sizes. You can record some of those shapes on paper with crayon rubbings. Collect them! Trade them! Show them to your friends!

- Old newspapers
- Paper
- Crayons with the wrapper peeled off.
- Green leaves, small flowers, any plants whose shapes you like.

~NEXT~

Step 1 Spread the newspaper out on the table.

Step 2 Lay down the leaves, plants or flowers.

Step 3 Place the paper over the leaves or plants.

Step 4

Lightly rub over the leaves or plants with the side of a crayon.

Step 5

The image of the leaf or flower will appear on your paper.

You can make patterns by laying leaves and flowers in circles, squares, etc. You can also make rubbings on tree bark, or for you brave souls, old tombstones. Make sure you have permission.

Look! A Book

You can be an author and make your own book using a few simple items. Use your book to collect your writings, leaf rubbings, and artwork.

You will need these items

- Several brown paper bags
- A ruler
- Twine or yarn
- Scissors
- A hole punch

Step 1
Cut open brown paper bags with the scissors.

Step 2
Cut the bags into flat, square pieces that are all the same size. (Use your ruler.) These will be your book pages.

Step 3
Stack the pages together.

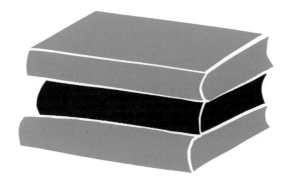

Step 4 Punch holes about 1/2 inch (1.2 centimeters) apart along one edge of the pages.

Step 5 Thread twine or yarn through the holes to stitch the book together.

If you know how to use a sewing machine or know someone who does, sew the edge of the pages together. Once you have your book, you can glue in pictures or write on the pages.

One Last Note

The projects in this book are just a few of the infinite ways that you can express yourself through arts and crafts. No matter what problems the world has, we will always need the arts. Art shows us the world in a different light and makes us feel better about ourselves. So be creative, use your imagination, and most importantly — have fun!

Glossary

Ancient — Belonging to times long past.

Artist — A person skilled in painting, sculpture, or literature.

Author — A person who writes books, poems, or stories.

Chemical — An element or compound used for producing a chemical effect.

Collage — A picture made by pasting on a background such things as parts of photographs, newspapers, fabric and string.

Dyes — A substance that can be mixed with water and used to color cloth.

Fiber — A slender and long natural or synthetic thread.

Gourd — The fruit of a vine whose hard, dried shell is used for cups, bowls, or ornaments.

Landfill — An area built up by burying layers of trash between layers of dirt.

Microscope — An instrument with a lens for making small things look larger.

Minerals — A substance obtained by mining or digging in the earth.

Oxygen — An element that is found in the atmosphere as a colorless, odorless, tasteless gas.

Paraffin — A waxy flammable substance used for making candles.

Plastic — A man-made material that can be molded and shaped when heated.

Recycle — To treat or process something in order that it may be used again.

Soil — The upper layer of the Earth in which plants grow.

Styrofoam — A flexible form of plastic that has many uses, not biodegradable.

Toxic — Harmful or poisonous.

Connect With Books

Chaote, Judith and Green, Jane. *Scrapcraft.* Garden City, New York: Doubleday & Company, Inc., 1973.

Eckstein, Artis Aleene. *How to Make Treasures from Trash.* Great Neck, New York: Hearthside Press, Inc., 1972.

Lohf, Sabine. *Nature Crafts.* Chicago: Children's Press, 1990.

Razzi, James. *Bag of Tricks.* New York: Parents' Magazine Press, 1971.

Schuman, Jo Miles. *Art From Many Hands.* Worcester, Massachusetts: Davis Publications, Inc., 1981.

Time-Life Books. *Creative Projects Big and Small.* Alexandria, Virginia, 1988.

Index

TARGET EARTH™

COMMITMENT

At Target, we're committed to the environment. We show this commitment not only through our own internal efforts but also through the programs we sponsor in the communities where we do business.

Our commitment to children and the environment began when we became the Founding International Sponsor for Kids for Saving Earth, a non-profit environmental organization for kids. We helped launch the program in 1989 and supported its growth to three-quarters of a million club members in just three years.

Our commitment to children's environmental education led to the development of an environmental curriculum called Target Earth™ aimed at getting kids involved in their education and in their world.

In addition, we worked with Abdo & Daughters Publishing to develop the Target Earth™ Earthmobile, an environmental science library on wheels that can be used in libraries, or rolled from classroom to classroom.

Target believes that the children are our future and the future of our planet. Through education, they will save the world!

TARGET®

Minneapolis-based Target Stores is an upscale discount department store chain of 517 stores in 33 states coast-to-coast, and is the largest division of Dayton Hudson Corporation, one of the nation's leading retailers.